The Life and Adventures of Capt. John Avery, the Famous English Pirate, (rais'd From a Cabbin-boy, to a King) now in Possession of Madagascar.

The *Life* and *Adventures* of Capt. *John*

Avery the Famous *English* Pirate, (rais'd from a Cabbin-Boy, to a King) now in Possession of *Madagascar*

Giving a distinct Account of his Birth, Parentage, Education, Misfortunes, and Subsequent exploits. His leaving the Government on Board the *Resolution* and *Nonsuch* Men of War The Reasons why he quitted that Service, for that of the Merchants. His putting to Sea in a Merchant Ship, where he drew in the Crew to turn Pirates with him His failing to *Jamaica*, where he disposed of the Ship's Cargo His taking a large Ship, worth above a Million Sterling, belonging to the Great *Mogu*, with his Grand Daughter on Board, who was going to be marry'd to the King of *Persia* attended by a great Retinue of Ladies. His Marriage with the said Princess, and his Men with her Retinue The Methods he took to establish himself. His Wealth, Strength, and Acquisitions by Sea and Land His Character The several Overtures he has made to return to his Obedience. A Description of the Country, with its Customs, Manners, &c Written by a Person who was on the Ledge from thence, and faithfully extracted from his Journal

The PREFACE.

AS Prefaces are necessary, when the Credit of any Memoirs is liable to be call'd in Question, so it may not be improper to give the Reader one at this Juncture, who, from the many Impostures of this Nature, will be apt to suspend his Belief concerning Things so remotely transacted, and Persons so obscure and imperceptible in their Practice. Who is this person! asks one, that made his Escape from *Madagascar* says one. How came he to be let into the Captain's inmost Secrets? cries another An easy way to get rid of a Liberty concerning a Writer that is justly said, by the like Liberty takes a Privilege in concluding all they like this, which is reach'd is own by that Purchase, and hits him a Kick in the Breech, to like a severe he his Faculty of Feeling To gratify such curious Reader as these, and prepossess the Publick against all Manner of scruptions Objections, is to know, that the Author of this small Treatise, is one Adrian Van Brock, a Dutch Gentleman, who after a very liberal Education at Leyden, with drew himself, as Most of the best Persons in Holland do, to the Business of Trade. This settlement, which he made to the satisfaction of all that he acts with and he who was to the Governors of the Dutch East-India Company, who in order to one so much Interest also to Surinan cargo to one of their outward ships, very richly laden, and for the ship with Letters recommendatory for a profitable Employ, when he should arrive at Batavia. But Fortune, that is not always in Friendship with those who deserve suffer'd this Ship to spring a Leak, and founder it Sea, near the Island of St Helena, though the Crew made their Escape in their Pinnace and long Boat Among the rest, Adrian Van Brock, who had lost very considerably of his own by this Disaster, came ashore, and after Application to the Governor, got another Ship upon the Company's Account, and so made the best of his Way for Batavia. Yet, notwithstanding the Danger he had just before escap'd from, and the Treasure the Type of Inconstancy had made the roaring Sea rob him of, he was to fall under another Disappointment more severe then the former, which was, to be intercepted in his voyage by Pirates, that were some of Capt. Avery's Band, and after plundering him ready Money, which consisted of some thousand Dollars, brought him, and

A

his Ship and Company, into Madagascar, where being Lad before the Captain to be examin'd about his Circumstances, and the Affairs of Europe, the Captain contracted such an Esteem for him, as was only to offer him a free Residence, but such a Share in his new erected Government, as he should think fit to accept of Van Broek was by no Means to show his Displeasure and ill Will by a Devil, wherefore he laid hold of his Offer, and was admitted into his most secret Thoughts, which gave him Occasion to know such a Part of these Memoirs, as his Birth, Education, Marriage, &c. which he was not an Eye-Witness to But as generous and liberal Spirits cannot long down with dishonourable Practices, so this Gentleman could no longer brook an Abode amongst this Nest of Thieves, than Necessity requir'd it; and laying Hold of the English East-India Men, whom the Sequel of these Memoirs will tell us to be dismiss'd in Safety, with a Letter to the Governor of Port St. George, he got on Board with his Effects, which consisted of Money which Avery had plentifully stor'd him with, by Stealth in the Night-Season, and so after staying some Time in the English Settlements, got safely to Batavia, where he now lives possess'd of a very good Post, which he was before recommended to. What remains after this, is, to answer some Objections which may be made to the Truth of it, from his mentioning nothing of this in the Body of the Memoirs, and this may be done by referring the Reader to the best Writers of this Kind, such as Cæsar in his Commentaries, &c. who industriously pass over what relates to themselves, unless an absolute Necessity requires it Besides, it would very much take off from the Opinion of our Author's Judgment and Qualifications, to introduce any Thing relating to himself, in a History that treats of nothing but unjustifiable Principles and Practices. To keep the Reader no longer from entering into the House, by detaining him in the Porch, he has nothing to do, but to go in and make himself welcome; where, though he will find no Dainties or Luxuriance of Stile to feed upon, he'll have that the Gods themselves were pleas'd with at a homely Entertainment at Baucis's and Philemon's, if the Poet saith Truth, by his Super ann vultus accessere boni.

The Life and Adventures of Capt. John Avery, &c.

AS Truth is more necessary towards enlightening Matters purely historical, than the Embellishments of Stile; and a naked Simplicity more suits this *Truth*, than those ornamental Advantages which are wanting to set off Falsehoods and romantick Relations, the Writer of these Memoirs, who is perfectly well known to the Person that gives Being to 'em, has thought fit to entertain his Reader with none of those Flourishes our modern Annalists and Historians abound with, but without assuming to himself any of their Airs, lay Things before him without any other Dress, than the Gentleman he is now going to treat, had when his Mother first brought him into the World.

Capt. John Avery was born at *Plymouth*, a noted Sea-Port Town in *Devonshire*, in the Year 1653. and rather descended from Parents noted for their Industry, than Birth His Father had spent several Years of his Life in the Service of the Crown, with his Fellow Townsman Admiral *Blake*; but meeting with little Encouragement, and finding a total Defection from the Royal Cause in the Beginning of the late civil War, chose rather to abandon his dear Friend and Country-man, than his sovereign Lord, he betook himself to the Merchants, under whom, by his prudent and careful Demeanor, he got a competent Estate, and the Reputation of a very able Sea-man. His Mother, who had the Care of the young Infant during her Husband's Absence in foreign Parts, was not behind hand with him in her Industry at Home, but took such Care of the Son, as might one Day render him possess'd of the Abilities of his Fa ther ; but unfortunately dying while her Husband was at Sea, and her Son in the 6th Year of his Age, left him to the Direction of a Sister of her's, one Mrs *Norris* who was an Inhabitant of the same Town with her. This Aunt of his, who was a Widow, and had no Children of her own, surpass'd the Mother (if it was possible) in Tokens of Affection , and finding him of a very forward Genius, took such Care of his Education, as was proper for a Child of whom she had conceiv'd such promising Hopes , and having put him to School, had the Satisfaction not only of seeing him out-strip those of his own Years, but those that had been born some Years before him But here, is if *Fate* pointed out the Grandeur and Wealth which should in Process of Time (unfortunately) arrive at, he gave Indications of such a daring and commanding Genius, as made some of his little School-Fellows very uneasy, and give in many Complaints against him, for his tyrannical Treatment Tho' their Complaints were to no Purpose, *Nature* had eradicated in him a Thirst of Empire, and Obedience to his Superiors, was as little consonant to his Character, as a moderate and obliging Behaviour to his Inferiors The Master heard and saw all this, and chastis'd him to no Purpose. At last, the Father return'd Home, and being content with the Fortunes he had happily acquir'd, wisely resolv'd to tempt the Inconstancy of the Seas no more, but to cast Anchor in a Port that would render him secure from all the Danger the Winds and Waves had before threaten'd him with To put these Resolutions in Practice, he purchas'd upwards of 160 *l.* a Year, near *Plymouth*, at a Place call'd *Cat-Down*, a Sort of an Eminence over-Looking an Arm of the Sea , which, by its various *Meanders* and Windings, runs several Miles into the Country, and takes its Name from a Mountain or Down, which at once swells above, and defends it from the Insults of tempestuous Weather.

Here the brave old Man took up his Residence , and after having liv'd to see the Royal Family restor'd in the Person of the augult Monarch, King *Charles* the IId, and his Country deliver'd from the Usurpations it had tyrannically labour'd under for many Years, sung his *nunc dimittis*, and gave up his Soul, *Mar.* 14, 1663, into the Hands of him that gave it him Now was our young Pirate just entering into the eleventh Year of his Age, and once more under the immediate Care of his Aunt, who was appointed of his Guardian, together with Mr. *Bartholomew Knowles*, a Sea-faring Person, who was equally rich with old *Avery*, but not equally honest, as the Sequel will give us to understand. His Aunt liv'd with him under the Capacity of a Tutoress for about four Years, when being of a very great Age, she gave Way to the Declensions of Nature, and paying Obedience to the Laws of Mortality, left this World, and him possess'd of 500 *l*, more than he had before her Decease.

Mr. *Knowles* being now sole Executor, and those Impediments remov'd by his Aunt's Death, which hinder'd him from putting those evil Designs in Practice, which he had long projected ; what does he to compass them, but by giving Way to those Inclinations he saw most predominant in his *Ward*, encourage him in his Desires to go aboard a Fleet of Men of War, that was then going to suppress the Nest of Pirates at *Algiers*. *Avery*, for his Part, took this as an Earnest of his Indulgence , and being vested with the Character of a Reformade by the King's Letter, he set Sail from *Plymouth* with the Squadron that was order'd out for the Purposes before-mention'd , where we shall leave him, to see how his Guardian bestow'd his Time in his Absence, who husbanded it as well as Villany could instruct him, by the following Method There was a neighbouring Attorney, with whom he had contracted an intimate Acquaintance, (I will not say Friendship, for that's an Appellation no Ways familiar to Men of evil Dispositions and Characters) and who had as true a Taste as himself of Things for-

A 2 bidden

bidden by the Laws of God and Man This Backslider, *in noverna Universis*, knew as well how to forge Deeds, as his Brother in Iniquity how to persuade him to it, and it took not up much Labour, but Conveyances were made, and other Instruments drawn, which entitled *Knowles* to the Possession of the Estate at *Cat-Down*, exclusive of the lawful Proprietor A hundred Pounds for his Pains, removed all Difficulties, and neither the Violation of Things sacred and civil, after such a delicate Morsel, put the least Rub in his Way As for the 500 *l.* he had no Manner of Consultation about getting of them into his Hands, they were already in 'em, and a good round Bill of Charges would soon make him Master of that Sum, without any Fear of the Equity of his Ward's Pretences. In the mean while, young *Avery* shews an uncommon Readiness in the Practice of Maritime Affairs, and not only gets into the Esteem of the Officers of his Majesty's Ship the *Resolution*, which he serv'd aboard, but of the Commodore Rear Admiral *Lawson*, and having exerted an extraordinary Vigor and Sprightliness while *Algiers* was reduc'd to Reason by the Terror of the *English* Navy, begg'd of his Captain to let him serve in the same Quality as he did in his Ship, aboard another Vessel that was order'd with three more to be detach'd for the *West Indies*, where the *Spaniards* began to be troublesome to our foreign Plantations, which was immediately granted him, as a Token of good Will that Commander bore him, and an Encouragement to his future Progress in the Art of Navigation But I must not carry him from aboard the *Resolution*, to the *Nonsuch*, (for that was the Ship he was to go to the *Indies* in) before I give the remarkable Occurrence which claims a Share in this History, which is this It being a Custom for the Reformades, especially those which are most in the good Graces of the commanding Officer, to dine with the Captain, it was his good Fortune to be one of 'em, while they were taking in Provision at the Port of *Cadiz*, and the second Lieutenant of the Ship being then invited also to Table, they fell to Gaming, as is usual, for want of other Diversion, after Dinner, and our young Tarpawlin had the Fortune to strip this Officer of the ready Money he was Master of, and would not play with him after, as he was desir'd, upon Honour. This enrag'd the Lieutenant to the last Degree, who vow'd Revenge, not being able to accomplish it in the Captain's Presence, where no Breach of the Peace was to be committed, and the profoundest Respect was due He therefore took Occasion next Morning to shew his Resentment by a Bastinado, for a pretended Neglect in the Reformade's not doing his Duty, who not being able to brook a Blow, that was given him so undeservedly, having watch'd the Lieutenant ashore, got Leave of his Officer likewise to have the Boat mann'd out and go ashore, where he found his Antagonist, and after calling him to Account for Satisfaction, had it in wounding him in several Places, for which he was confin'd at his returning on Board again, for some Time, but afterwards dismiss'd with Applause, for his gallant Behaviour, when his Captain came to be inform'd of the true State of the Case.

We have no Room to question, but this fortunate and daring Adventure flush'd him with Expectation of Success in his future Encounters, and gave Additions to a Courage that stood in need of no Access to it But to be as concise as we can in our Narration, without Digressions by Way of Remarks, let it suffice, that we bring him in the Commodore's Ship before *Port Royal* in *Jamaica* where, being of an active Genius, while the Vessels of War were careening he grew impatient of some other Exploit, and put himself aboard a Buccaneer who was going in Quest of Plunder, and was so fortunate as to return to *Jamaica* with some Ingots of Gold and Silver to his share ; but as he was of an unpositive Temper, it did not long stay with him but went among the Inhabitraits, to make appear, that he was not only a perfect Sailor in the Knowledge of Things relating to the Sea, but also very readily vers'd in the Practices of those that use it, upon the Account he was then embark'd in

Here he stay'd cruizing and securing the Commerce in those Seas, for the Space of two Years, when the Commodore being recall'd Home, he was oblig'd to set Sail for his Country; at which he was no sooner arriv'd, but he found his Guardian dead, and himself dispossess'd not only of his Estate, but Aunt's Legacy, by a pretended Deed of Conveyance, and full of Charges. Whom to have Recourse to in these Extremities, he knew not. At last, having receiv'd the Pay that was due to him from the Ship, he commenc'd a Suit against Knowles his Executors, but all to no Purpose, for what by the Treachery of his own Lawyers, and what by the Prejudice of the Judges in his Adversary's Favour, he found himself under the Necessity of going to Sea again, by losing his Favour. And here an Opportunity offer'd for his being employ'd, and reveng himself upon his Country's Enemies, for the Perfidies of his pretended Friends King Charles the IId had declar'd War against the Dutch for several Incroachments on his Royal Prerogative, and a Fleet was going to Sea to do his Majesty Justice for those Injuries. Among the Rest that made Application for Preferment on this Occasion, Avery was one that attended the Board of Admiralty, but his Fortunes being lost, his former Favours were vanish'd also, and though he had serv'd so long under a more genteel Character, he found himself oblig'd to submit to a Fore-mast-man's Place aboard the Edgar, where he continu'd during that whole War in no other Capacity, than having the Satisfaction of being serviceable to his King and Country

When both Parties were weary of fighting, they began then more seriously to enter into the Causes of their Enmity, which not being thought sufficient to justify it on either Side, occasion'd a Treaty of Peace between two Nations, that had been beaten enough to make 'em take Care how they fell together by the Ears for the future. This returns our Champion back again of Course to the Place of his Nativity, where having some Interest, tho' he had none with the Council to his Royal Highness the Duke of York, then Lord High Admiral, he prevail'd with some Merchants of Totnes and Plymouth, upon a Ship's being bound for the West Indies, to be her Commander, and was so fortunate in her, as to perform several Voyages for his Owners, with all imaginable Success. The Places he traded to for the Merchants, were chiefly the Leeward Island, but his Genius being active and enterprizing, he was loth to sit farther, and went to the Bay of Campechy, where he cut down a considerable Quantity of Log-wood, traffick'd with the Spaniards, and return'd Home with a very rich Cargo. The Merchants look'd upon him as a busy and bold Commander, his Courage had been try'd upon several Occasions, and his Conduct been render'd irreproachable, thro' the many happy Results of it, as all his Behaviour was with as much Gallantry as could be expected from the most resolute Sailor on the Ocean. Nor did he, by several other Acts of Prudence and Justice, miss of their Esteem, who trusted and employ'd him; for indeed, to speak impartially of this Captain, he had been worthy of a very great Character, if he had made Use of those excellent Qualities, which he was in an eminent Manner Master of, for the Benefit of his Country, as he afterwards manag'd them for its Disadvantage

'Tis with a great deal of Address and Difficulty, that some very able Politicians make themselves belov'd and esteem'd by those they have a Design upon, but Capt. Avery, without the least Uneasiness, had the Art of gaining the Affections of the Mariners, and shewing his Authority, without weakening their Inclinations for his having the Exercise of it, nay, our better Sort of Tarpawlins

A 3

lins, that lay'd Claim to more diftinguifhing Apprehenfions, view'd their Images, and doated upon themfelves in the Survey of this He was, as to his Proportion, indic'te-fiz'd, inclurable to be fat, and of a gay jolly Complexion. His Manner of living, was imprinted in his Face, and none that faw him, but might have eafily tel his Profeffion, without making Application to *John Partridge*, *Ifaac Bickerftaff*, or any other Aftrologer in *Chriftendom*, for a Scheme to know it by His Temper was of a Piece with his Perfon, daring and good-humour'd, if not provok'd, but infolent, uneafy, and unforgiving to the laft Degree, if at any Time impos'd upon His Knowledge in Affairs relating to his Calling, was grounded upon a ftrong natural Judgment, and a fufficient Experience, that was highly advanc'd by an inceffant Application to the Mathematicks, and notwithftanding the Remiffnefs of his Education and Converfe in his Minority, he had many Principles of Morality, which, fince his Defection from an equitable Procedure, feveral of the Subjects belonging to the Crown of *Great Britain*, have fufficiently experienc'd.

Thefe Vertues, both natural and acquir'd, gain'd him a Reputation with the moft intelligent Perfons, that either appli'd themfelves to Navigation, or had Dealings with thofe that did, and the moft accurate in their Projections, had an Eye upon him, as one that might advance as far upon the Surface of the Ocean, and make as fignal Difcoveries, as his Predeceffors, the Admirals *Drake* and *Hawkins*, who ufed to be, like him, been Inhabitants of *Plymouth*, and were rais'd from no higher Beginnings, than our modern Adventurer But Fate had decreed it otherwife, and he was juft upon the Point of feeing himfelf a Great Man by honeft Practices, when an unlucky Accident fhipwreck'd his good Fortune, and occafion'd his being enroll'd in the Lift of Robbers himfelf, who had not long fince been plunder'd of his Patrimony, by bafe and indirect Meafures

It happen'd, that among other Paffions he was fubject to, that of Love was not the leaft, and he had pitch'd his Eyes upon a Farmer's Daughter, as one that would make him happy in matrimonial Enjoyments after his Return from Sea, from which thofe Pleafures avert their Face, and as his Circumftances were as agreeable to the Parents, as his Appearance to the Daughter, the Portion was agreed upon, and they were both marry'd, (as every one thought) to their mutual and lafting Contentment. Tho' it prov'd, that the Farmer was none of the honefteft, as his Daughter happen'd afterwards to fall under the Character of none of the chafteft, for the firft took Advantage of his Son-in-Law's taking a Sword for his Daughter's Portion, and refus'd to pay him one Farthing, the laft was hopefully brought to Bed of a champion Boy, fix Months after the Bridal Night, as much like a certain Inn-keeper in the Town, as if it had been fpit out of his Mouth. 'Tis eafy to imagine fuch Difappointments as thefe, were enough to fet a Temper on Fire, that was too fanguine to pocket fuch Abufes, wherefore, having withdrawn his Effects from *Plymouth*, and made ready Money of all he was Mafter of, he made the beft of his Way for *London*, and gave a plain Indication, at his Arrival there, that as Hatred and Averfion make us bloody-minded, fo they teach us to diffemble, while he difguis'd his Thoughts in order to put them more mifchievoufly in Execution.

Here he had no fooner made the proper Reflexions on his Misfortunes, and heartily curs'd the Authors of his Ruin, according to ancient Cuftom, but he put on very honeft undefigning Looks, and apply'd himfelf once more to fome Merchants, whofe Service he had been formerly engag'd in, and for whom *he* had made many a fuccefsful Voyage. He pretended a more than ordinary Defire of repairing his Loffes by Trade; and to that Purpofe affur'd them, that he would not only venture all the ready Monies he was already poffefs'd of, but

whatever

whatever Goods his Stock of Reputation could purchase, after the unhappy Accidents that had befallen him. Which Proposals were readily clos'd with, and the Gentlemen apply'd to, not only fitted him out a Ship of 400 Tuns, ready mann'd, victuall'd, and freighted, but gave him Credit for several hundred Pounds, and made him Supercargo, as well as Commander. This was as he could have wish'd, and the War that was declar'd and in France raging at that Time, it afforded Capt. Avery a fair Opportunity of providing his Ship with a far greater Number of Guns and Men, than at any other Time would have appear'd necessary. Neither did the Pains he took to procure able Sailors upon this Occasion, and such as were remarkable for their Courage give any Manner of Suspicion to the Owners, but out he sail'd with as bold a Crew, as ever trusted themselves to Wind and Weather.

His first Exploit, after he had got Sea-Room, was, to sound the Inclination of his Men, for nothing was to be done without their Concurrence. He lay'd before 'em the frequent Hazards they were oblig'd to run, for no valuable Consideration. That if they would permit him to lead them on, he promis'd one Day's resolute Fight should make the Residue of their Lives an uninterrupted Scene of Pleasure. That it was mere Madness to depend on the Merchants, who suffer'd the bravest Fellows to grow old, low, and miserable in their Service, without having any Regard to their Labours. That it was an equal Frenzy, to hazard all for the Government, whereof, as he had personally experienc'd, Promotion seldom attended true Merit, where the Insolence of Commanders was insufferable, and where the Tarpawlins of Honour had nothing to expect for the Reward of their Wounds and Bravery, but a poor Apartment in an unprovided Hospital, when Age and ill Usage had render'd 'em unfit for further service. With these, and such like Arguments, drawn from the unfortunate Management of the Navy in those Days, and by perswading his Men, that they should meet with Mines richer than those of Potosi, he so far prevail'd with 'em, that one and all, they determin'd to adhere to his Resolutions. Thus, being again satisfy'd with their Consent to his Design, he forthwith made the best of his Way to the Island of Juanne, where he was not a little acquainted, (as the Reader has been before given to understand) and there dispos'd of that Part of the Ship's Cargo which would be of no Use to him in his intended Voyage. But an unlucky Accident had like to have marr'd his Project, and blasted a Design which he had conceiv'd so hopeful an Opinion of, for the Person whom he had chosen for his Clerk and Steward, being appriz'd of the Matter, and puff'd up with the Expectation of a great Reward for the Discovery, had made an Agreement with one of the Ship's Crew, who was the Gunner's Mate, to go ashore the next Day, and make it known to Sir William Beeston, who was then Governor, but the Fellow whom this Resolution was concerted with, had some Remorse amidst his Wine of it, and communicated the whole Secret to the Captain, who laid an Embargo on his trusty Servant, 'till they were out at Sea, and then decently truss'd him up, for being a Traytor to his trayterous and piratical Purposes.

Being victuall'd afresh, he incited some Persons, who had been Buccaneers, to join him, and with all imaginable Expedition, set Sail to cruize in the Indian Sea, where, after an Oath taken of every individual Mariner, for Secrecy in the Affair they were going in Pursuit of, he tack'd about backwards and forwards for a considerable Time, before any Prize of Value came in Sight. At last, Fortune, that intended to make him miserable, by being reputed happy, threw in his Way a Vessel of a great Burthen, for she carry'd near a thousand Men, with Guns proportionable, was freighted with the richest Merchandizes of all the East, and had got a Prize of greater Value about her, I mean a Grand-Daughter of Aureu-

zek, who was then Great Mogul, and commanded an Empire almost as exten-
five as any known Quarter of the World. The Force of the Ship, and the vaſt
Numbers of Soldiers that appear'd on its Deck, at firſt gave no ſmall Uneaſi-
neſs to Capt *Avery*, who was loath to miſcarry in his firſt Attempt, and ſeem'd
doubtful of Succeſs at the ſame Time as he was ſet on Tip-toe to proſecute it,
but having recollected himſelf, he conſider'd his own Strength, the Bravery of
his Seamen, and their wonderful Skill in naval Rencounters, while the Numbers of the others would rather be a Hinderance to 'em, than an Advantage,
and the Wan of being unexercis'd in military Affairs, render'd them as weak
as they were numerous, therefore he gave Orders for the Signal of Battel, and
immediately commanded to bear down upon the *Indians*, and exerted ſuch a Courage, as if he had prophetically known, that the Reward of his Victory ſhould
be the moſt charming of the fair Sex, and the moſt precious of all ineſtimable
Things that the Iſle could preſent him with

The *Enemy* gave but a Broadſide or two, when the *Indians* ſtruck their Colours, and reſign'd themſelves to the Mercy of their Enemies. The Cargo of
this Ship was ſo very rich, that it even ſatiated the Appetites of the moſt covetous of the Mariners, for above the Value of a Million of Money in Silver and
rich Stuffs, was found therein, and a very agreeable Lady into the Bargain The
Captain no ſooner beheld the Lady in Tears, but melted into Compaſſion, forgot
thoſe inhuman Reſolutions he had taken at his Departure from *England*, and being of an amorous Diſpoſition, notwithſtanding his Wife had ſerv'd him the
ſcurvy Trick before-mention'd, inſtead of raviſhing the Princeſs, which ſome
Accounts have made mention of, pay'd the Reſpect that was due to her high
Birth, took her and her Attendance into his own Ship, and after deſpoiling the
Veſſel of all its Wealth, ſuffer'd it and its Crew to ſteer on to their intended Port
It ſeems the Riches of the Ship was deſign'd as a Portion for the Princeſs, and
was ſent as a Preſent to a *Perſian* Potentate, who never had the Fortune to enjoy
the glittering Cargo, nor his intended Spouſe, for the Captain had plunder'd
her of ſomething more pleaſing than the Jewels, tho' not without her Conſent,
and being join'd in Marriage, after the Cuſtom of thoſe Foreigners, for he had
a Prieſt with her, who did that Office after her Country's Manner, and *Avery*
was e'en contented to diſmiſs the Scruples of his being marry'd after the Church
of *England* Method, out of Complaiſance to ſo deſireable a Creature. The reſt
of the Ship's Crew drew Lots for her Servants, and to follow the Example of
their Commander, even ſtay'd their Stomachs till the ſame Prieſt had ſaid Grace
for them, that did it for their Maſter, when they fell to as heartily, as if they
were to feaſt after that Rate no more during their Lives, and being full of
Wealth, when they were almoſt empty of Love, came in Sight of the Iſland of
Madagaſcar

This Exploit of theirs having reach'd the Mogul's Ears in a ſhort Time after,
he immediately cauſed 30000 Men to advance towards the *Engliſh* Settlements,
by Way of Repriſals, but the *India*-Company being appriz'd of his Reſentments,
ſtopt his Anger with Preſent, 'till they could give Notice to their Correſpon-
dents in *England*, who bought Dr *D——nt* a fine Gown to appear in before their
Ambaſſador at the Mogul's Court But the Doctor was either too fearful to venture his Carcaſs where it might not be fed, or too intent on a Place which he
had in View at Home, to go ſo far to ſeek for it Abroad, tho' Sir *William Norris*
bravely accepted the Employment, and went thro' it with a Courage peculiar to
his heroick Family. The Mogul, at his Arrival into his Territories, not only
defray'd his Charges, but ſent him Home with rich Preſents, tho' he had the
Misfortune to die in his Return thither, and not bring 'em Home to his Family

ly in Perſon, which ſhews, that a covetous Prince minds Money more than Conſanguity, and makes the Maxim good, *That Princes have no Relations, while either the Extent of their Territories are concern'd, or the Augmentation of their Treaſures.*

To return to *Madigaſcar*, where we left our triumphant Heroe and Lover, with the reſt of his Adventurers. They were no ſooner in Sight of the Iſland, but whole Troops of Inhabitants came down to the Shore, in order to take a Survey of the Ship, and the People he brought with him. The Captain was ſomewhat ſtartl'd at ſo numerous an Appearance, but being told of the Fertility of the Iſland by ſome of the Buccaneers, and the Diſpoſition of its Inhabitants, ſent ſome of 'em with a Flag of Truce, and Preſents for their chief Commanders, who no ſooner receiv'd them, but with Expreſſions of Joy after their Way, conducted 'em to their King. This Prince's Reſidence was about three Miles off from the Shore, which was ſurrounded, after the Manner of the *Eaſtern* People, and made up of great Numbers of Huts. Here they found drawn up in a Semicircle about 1000 arm'd Men, and in the Midſt of 'em ſat down on a Carpet croſs-legg'd three Perſons, who ſeem'd ſuperior to the reſt by their Habit and Looks. The Middlemoſt was the chief, and the other two that ſat at a convenient Diſtance on each Side of him, his Brother, and prime Miniſter of State. The Freebooters were no ſooner come in Sight, but the little Army made a diſmal Cry, and brandiſh'd their Spears in the Air, in a ſeemingly threatening Poſture, which they underſtood afterwards by Means of an Interpreter, was deſign'd as a Welcome to Court. In an Inſtant, all was Attention and Silence, and 2 or 3 Officers of State ſtept out of their Ranks to conduct the Pirates to Audience, who having paid their Reſpects in their Country Manner, told him, The Occaſion of their coming into thoſe Parts, was, for the Wealth and Advantage of the Country, that their Commander was a very powerful and great Man, and having receiv'd ſome Laws from the Potentates of Europe, was in Search of a Place convenient, from whence he might moleſt 'em in the moſt ſenſible Part, which was, that of Trade; and that his Arrival in thoſe Parts, would not only make him a Prince would be to his Neighbours, but all the World would come into an Alliance with him, and deſire to make Settlements in his Territories. His Majeſty, after having, in reply, by his chief Miniſter, the Purport of their Errand, gave them in anſwer, that an Alliance with ſo great a Commander, would be very welcome, and that he himſelf would, after due Preparations for his Reception, go in Perſon and attend him to Court, and having given Orders for their Entertainment, in which was his great Satisfaction in the Preſent, which were the Ladies, rode up, and retir'd, as is uſual with the Oriental Princes, to convert them their Wives.

In the mean Time, Capt. *Avery*, to loſe no Time, ſet all Hands at work in forming the Bay on the *Eaſt* Side of this Iſland, in 15 Degrees 30 Minutes *South* Latitude, which was large and capacious, and unexpos'd to the Fury of the moſt tempeſtuous Weather. Towards the Bottom of it lies a ſmall Iſland about ten Miles in Circumference, whoſe Land round it being high and woody, makes it a ſure Protection for all Veſſels which anchor'd but a-ſtern; and here he choſe to continue 'till the Return of his Meſſengers, who rode home the Report abovemention'd. The King of the Country, as is good as his Word in a Day or two after, and came very nobly attended to invite the Capt. on ſhore, who receiv'd him under a Diſcharge of all his Artillery, and with all the Reſpect due to a Perſon of the higheſt Character, and having entertain'd him and his Retinue with all Things the Ship afforded, which was of an aſtoniſhing Bulk to the Infidels, very frankly accepted of his Invitation and went aſhore, where he found a Treatment that was uncommon with Barbarians, and much higher offer'd, that he was not the only European that had touch'd upon thoſe Coaſts.

Here

(10)

Here the two Potentates (for we muſt after this Interview, ſhare the Government of this Side of the World between them) enter'd into a perpetual Alliance :
and having regal'd themſelves after an extraordinary Manner, ſtipulated to ſtand
by each other with all their Forces When the Captain return'd to his Ship, in
order to take Poſſeſſion of the Place which was intended for his Abode, and was
the Iſland we juſt now told the Reader of, and on which, after mooring his Veſſel, he landed with all his Crew; but ſuch as were abſolutely neceſſary to look
after her In the firſt Place, what he had to do, was to cauſe all the Plunder
he had got, to be brought aſhore, and take Care, that an exact Dividend ſhould
be made of the whole, according to the Law of Pirates, who, tho' they make
it their Buſineſs to prey on Perſons of a different Life and Converſation, yet a-
mong themſelves obſerve the ſtricteſt Rules of Juſtice. He had no ſooner diſ-
pos'd of his Affairs to the general Satisfaction, cur'd his ſick Men, and careen'd
his Veſſel, but he embark'd again, having left Part of his Crew with the Women
on Shore, to look after freſh Booty, and ſet Sail for the neighbouring Iſles, which
lay contiguous, and interſpers'd in thoſe Seas not rar from one another, ſome of
which were of dangerous Acceſs, others afforded convenient Harbours, but all of
'em in general were found to be ſtor'd with moſt Neceſſaries of Life, as what
were wanting ſeem'd rather deſign'd to oblige the Luxurious, than to anſwer the
Demands of a reaſonable Appetite. During this Cruize, in which he took two
Mooriſh Veſſels, and an *Engliſh Eaſt India* Ship, outward bound, and very richly laden, he had Time to conſider of his paſt Life and Conduct, and conſult
with himſelf for his future Safety. He debated what Courſe was moſt proper
for him to take, to return for *England* was dangerous, all the World were his
Enemies, and if he eſcap'd the Danger of the Seas on ſuch a Voyage, he had
Reaſon to believe he ſhould periſh aſhore. Theſe Reaſons induc'd him to be
fix'd in his Reſolves, to chuſe the Place he had left the Women and Plunder in,
for a Retreat, ſince none could be more proper than theſe very Iſles about which
he was then cruizing, their Situation being a Trade lying as it were between the Eaſt
and *Weſt India* Seas. Their Neighbourhood to ſeveral Spice Iſlands, the Civi-
lity of their Inhabitants, their Diſtance from *Europe*, and the Plenty of Proviſ-
ſions that were found therein, powerfully and commonly to ſettle here a Colony,
which ſeem'd to be ſecure enough from all the Attempts that the Univerſe could
make againſt it Reſolv'd upon this Meaſure, to avoid future Dangers, after
having taken another Prize, which was full of *French*-men, deſign'd for the
ſame Exploits he was then in Exerciſe of, he communicated his Thoughts not
only to his Ship's Crew, but ſuch of his Priſoners as were *Engliſh* or *French*,
and at the ſame Time aſſur'd them, that ſuch who diſlik'd his Propoſal, were at
Liberty to retire aboard one of the Ships which he would furniſh them with
The Captain's Generoſity was ſo very much applauded, that very few, either
Engliſh or *French*, except the Commanders of the *Eaſt India* Ship, and Part of
his Crew, made the laſt Offer their Choice The *French*, for their Parts, being
ſenſible that they were one and all in his Power, thought it rather Prudence to
ſhare his Fortune, than for him to make himſelf Maſter of theirs, and more
than ſupply'd the Room of thoſe Sailors that were for returning into their own
Countries, though moſt of the *Engliſh* tarry'd with their Commander, and
landed with all Materials neceſſary to build a Fort with, for their mutual
Defence. This they effected in a little Time, and having plac'd ſeveral great
Guns upon it, and forty eight Pieces of Cannon they had taken out of the *Eaſt
India* Ship, for the Security of their Perſons and Effects, and call'd it by the
Name of *Fort Avery*, in Honour of their Leader, but as Bulwarks and Artille-
ry were not able to preſerve this piratical Government, without Laws and In-
ſtitutions

stitutions necessary for its Well-being and Continuance, several new Custom
and Ordinances were propos'd, and consented to by the Generality of the Ro-
vers, conducive as they imagin'd necessary for the Preservation of their new State,
and *Avery* was with abundance of Ceremony chosen and confirm'd in the Dignity of being their Chief, with such a Power as the Doges or Dukes of *Venice*
and *Genoa* are now possess'd of.

After this Republick of Pirates had thus order'd all Things to their Satisfaction, those who had Leave to retire, were shipp'd for the *Western* Islands in one
of the *Moorish* Vessels, and part of *Avery*'s new Subjects remain'd upon the I-
sland, while the other weigh'd Anchor from thence, in Search of new Adventures, under the Command of Monf *de Sale*, who was not in Power to the
new Duke, who, for his part, with his other Companies, who had Women
for their Shares, gave himself up to the Caresses of his new Princess. As Time
obliterates the most deep Impressions of Sorrow, so the Lady was not long before she forgot the Pleasures of her Grand-father's Court, in the Joys of her own,
and found herself happily brought to Bed of a Son soon after her Husband's being invested with his new Dignity, while the Female Part of her Retinue were
no less backward in presenting their Husbands with the Fruits of their conjugal
Endearments. But tho' the Commander in chief, with a small Number of his
Followers, had these Advantages, the rest of 'em were Strangers to Venereal
Enjoyments, and being Masters of the same Passions, were under a Restraint of
being Strangers to the same Priviledges, wherefore it was resolv'd, *nemine con-
tradicente*, that a Supply should be granted for the Good of their new-modell'd
Government, and the first Voyage should be made in Quest of Women, to perpe-
tuate it by way of Generation, lest the Want of Assistants from that Sex, should,
in Process of Time, render it extinct by a Failure of Succession. Nor was *Fortune* averse to their Designs, the ship soon return'd with a Cargo of Ladies. 'Tis
true, their Complexion is none of the fairest, but *Necess* takes up with every
Thing, and when they were weary of these, 'twas in their Power to have
more at the same Price, it being the Custom of the Islands, and of that part of
the Continent of *Africa* which lay near, to barter for Wives as they do for Cat-
tel, and you might as easily purchase a young Virgin of her Parents, as a Tooth
of Ivory, both being the Commodities and Merchandize of those Countries, only
here lay the Difference, the Lady was of less Value than the Tooth.

Thus Capt. *Avery* and his Adherents, meeting with all they could in Reason
desire in that part of the World where they liv'd, resolv'd to make their constant
Residence, and by Force or Persuasion, oblige several *Europeans* to partake in
the Fortunes of their new-structur'd Commonwealth, and in a little Time *Fame*
so afflicted their Intentions, that several Pirates of all Nations came to settle
themselves under his Protection, and he saw himself in Possession of a Government larger than he could have imagin'd in the Infancy of his Adventures. By
this Accession of Strength, he not only enlarg'd his Territories, but made all the
neighbouring Princes his Tributaries. Towns were built, Communities establish'd, Fortifications built, and Entrenchments flung up, as render'd his Dominions impregnable and inaccessible by Sea and Land, and tho' Commadore *War-
ren* came into those Parts with a Squadron of Men of War, to drive 'em from
thence, he had the Mortification to see such Efforts not only hazardous, but im-
practicable, and to return Home without any other Effect, than dispersing a Pardon, which was embrac'd by few of the Captain's Adherents, because their Commander in Chief was excepted.

But as in all Constitutions and Bodies Politick, there are still some Members
that compose it, of different Inclinations, and who, sway'd by Ambition, or by-
ass'd

as'd by Diſſaffection, think themſelves capable of commanding the whole, and highly injur'd while they are made ſubſervient to a Power that is ſuperior to 'em; ſo it was with ae Sale, who, not being content to be ſecond, loſt his Life, with his Expectations, while he was attempting to befall. This Man was a brave and daring Officer, but not being content th..d..., had..ly ...d his Life, when he firſt made him his Priſoner, but alſo...ed him to be his Viceroy, as it were, and the next in Command under him, ...ld'd...for him to do Acts of Mercy and Compaſſion, with the higheſt Injuſtice and Cruelty. The Lady that fell to his Share for a Help-mate, was neither beautiful, like Cap. Avery's nor of high Extraction, and he could not caſt an Eye on the one, without having the utmoſt Averſion for the other. He made uſe of all the little Artifices he could, to make the other's Lady, acquainted with his Paſſion, but either ſhe had too much Generoſity for her Huſband's Friend and Deputy, or too little Know-ledge in the Art and Myſteries of Love, to be ſenſible of his Deſigns, without a more formal Declaration. Whether it was Ignorance or Addreſs in her, it is nothing to our Purpoſe, the more innocent ſhe appear'd to the French-Man, ſhe ſeem'd ſtill Miſtreſs of the more Charms, and he took Reſolutions to enjoy her, that were as fatal as his Love was criminal. The Captain's Abſence from the Place of his uſual Abode, on the Affairs of his Government, gave the Villain an Opportunity of being more ſedulous in his Addreſſes, and he laid hold of it with an Eagerneſs that ſhew'd how impatient he was of any Delay, as he took Time by the Forelock in the following Manner. As the Violence of his Paſſion had made him reſolute and intrepid, ſo the Deſpair of ſucceeding in his Amours by fair Means, made him wholly intent how to accompliſh his Deſires by foul, whatſoever ſhould be the Conſequence. But firſt he thought it a Piece of Diſcretion, to feel the Pulſe of his Country-men the French, to whom he addreſs'd himſelf by way of Compl...t, relating to the Tyranny of the Engliſh, who would Lord it o-ver 'em in a ſtrange manner, unleſs M..I do...effec..'ly reply'd, to hereent their exorbitant Increaſe of Power. He told them, that it was his...to ſiſt'ſible to thoſe who would make any Enquiry into his paſt and preſent Conduct, that Avery aim'd at a deſpotical and arbitrary Government; that ſuch Deſigns were deſtructive of the very Being of their Settlement; that it behov'd every well-meaning Perſon, eſpecially thoſe of the French Nation, who had been ſo long uſed to Conqueſts, to ſhake off a Yoke that would never...get rid of without their immediate taking Advantage of the Captain's Abſence; that it was then Turn to relieve the Guard, and do Duty at the Caſtle that Day, and they at this very Juncture not only had it in their Power to deliver themſelves from approaching Slavery, but upon any Terms with their Prince, whom they had highly offended by tranſgreſſing the Law of Nations, in taking ſuch unlawful Courſes as they were forc'd to under their preſent Circumſtances, that all the Riches of Avery, which were inconceivably great, were lodg'd in the Caſtle they were going to be poſſeſs'd of, and that beſides thoſe Riches, they might have im-menſe Treaſures for the Mogul in reſtoring his Grand-daughter, the Princeſs, from her unjuſt Confinement, and d'live-ng her into his Hands, which might be done by the Capture...To conclude, he conjur'd 'em, by the Honour of their Country, and the Reſpect they bore to him, their Commander, who had journey'd ſo many thouſand Leagues with 'em, to ſhew themſelves like Men, in order to be poſſeſs'd of ſo glorious a Reward; and for his Part, he would not only lead 'em on, but would be the laſt that ſhould ſee 'em on Board their own Anchorage, in their Return Home, after the Proſecution of ſo noble and equitable a Deſign. The Proſpect of Gain, the Hopes of having their Pardons, and the Return to their native Soil, were Arguments too perſwaſive not to make Impreſſions upon the Minds of Men, who, being accuſtom'd to the Acts of Barbarity, made no Scruple of falling into Mea-
ſures

tures that were confonant to it; wherefore they jointly, one and all, agreed to live and die with their Commander, and as foon as the Watch-Bell fhould found, after their being poffefs'd of the Caftle, to fall to, and plunder all they fhould find in their Way, and neither fpare Man, Woman, or Child, but the Princefs and her Family. But here, as before at *Jamaica*, Capt *Avery*'s good Genius was fuperior to his evil, and ftood by him once more, in Oppofition to his Enemies, tho' perhaps to referve him for greater Misfortunes, if he perfifts in the Courfe of Life he yet continues to take. One *Pickard*, of *de Sale*'s Crew, had been very much abus'd by him, baftinado'd, and under an Arreft frequently when on Board with him, befides incapable of returning to *France* again for other Crimes, as Murder and Inceft, fhould that of Piracy be forgiven him; wherefore, after having long fought for an Opportunity of Revenge, he could not but hug himfelf at the Thoughts of this, as an infallible Means to difpatch his Enemy. What does he therefore do, but makes to the Captain of the Guard, one *Richardfon*, a Cornifh man, and formerly *Avery*'s Lieutenant, and acquaints him with the intended Confpiracy, giving him to underftand, that unlefs he took fpeedy Meafure to prevent it, two Hours Time would bring about fuch a Turn of Affairs as would be the univerfable Ruin of their whole Colony. *Richardfon*, for his Part, was a prudent Man, and wifely entertain'd a true Senfe of the Danger which his Mafter's Affairs were going to be involv'd in, wherefore, the firft Thing he did, was, to difpatch a Meffenger to Capt *Avery*, with an Account of the Premifes, and to defire his fpeedy Return, promifing not only to fecure his pernicious Deputy, but not to admit any Recruits to relieve the Guard in the Caftle. All this was punctually perform'd, for *Avery* coming, as his ufual Cuftom was, to pay his Refpects to the Princefs about an Hour before the Guard was to be reliev'd, was immediately put under an Arreft, to his great Confufion. But as it was not enough to make a Seizure of his Perfon, without thofe of his Accomplices, he was to look out for Meafures futable to this End, which was happily accomplifh'd by his calling in a whole Ship's Crew of *Englifh*, who were juft come into Port with fuch Force. Thefe he difpos'd in fuch a Manner with thofe he had before in Garifon, fo as when the Recruit fhould come upon the Parade, to furround 'em on every Side, and either make 'em Prifoners, or cut 'em entirely off, but as Villains, never fo defperate in their horrid Contrivances, have a cowardly Difpofition of Soul when they come to Action, fo thefe, when they faw themfelves encompafs'd, and commanded to lay down their Arms, or expect no Quarter, made Choice to fubmit to the Laws of *Neceffity*, and were hurry'd to Prifon without any manner of Refiftance, where they are to ftay 'till the Captain's and his Council's Arrival, who were to pafs Sentence upon 'em anfwerable to their Demerits.

This was no fooner done, but the News of it fpread over the whole Ifland, and not a *French*-man could be feen in it, but was in Danger of his Life from the Indignation thofe of other Nations had conceiv'd againft 'em, and had it not been for an Order that was iffu'd out upon *Avery*'s Arrival, to prevent fuch inconfiderate and cruel Proceedings, they had found themfelves wholly extinct by a general Maffacre. But Forms of Juftice were to be made Ufe of even among thofe People, whofe Way of Living fhew'd 'em converfant with nothing but Injuftice, and *de Sale* and his Accomplices were brought upon their Tryals, where, being found guilty, they were every Man condemn'd to be empal'd alive, and their Eftates confifcated for the Ufe of th Government. Which fevere Execution was accordingly put in Practice, without any Remorfe on the Side of the unhappy Perfons, that while they were made the Objects of other Folks Terror, fhew'd no other Concern under their Sufferings, than for their Villanies not being

profperous.

prosperous. As Plots are for the Use and Confirmation of Governments, when unsuccessful, so is this highly to the Advantage of the Captain and his new Dignity; for not only vast Riches fell to him by the Forfeiture of these Conspirators, but the great Council of the Island agreed, one and all, to pass such wholesome Laws in his Favour, as rais'd him to a Pitch of Sovereignty not any ways inferior to the greatest Potentate:

'Twas not only most high Treason to contrive against his Person, but to speak little of his Authority; and he saw himself invested with a Power as despotick as one of the most arbitrary Principles could wish for, or the highest Ambition could have in View. But as, amidst all the Prosperities of Life, Reflexions on the short Duration of it, will sometimes intervene, and the Inclinations of Mankind are not so sunk in Vice, as to admit no Thoughts that border upon Vertue, so the Captain could not but lean after a Project of his own native Country, and the Desire of finishing the Remainder of his Days where he first had the Happiness of seeing the Light, which was increas'd by looking into his past Crimes, and a just Survey of what he must one Day answer for at a Heavenly Tribunal, tho' he found himself out of the Reach of one that was Earthly. These Considerations, which he found himself more and more subject to, induc'd him to make Application to the East India Company trading to the East Indies, for Pardon, and having an Opportunity by one of their Ships, which was then brought in, and which he order'd to be immediately releas'd with great Civilities, he wrote the following Letter to Capt. Pitts, the Governor of Fort St George.

S I R,

THE Bearer can testify my Respects to the Company, by bringing you this, and whatever my Demeanor has been to other Nations, you may always rest assur'd of my particular Deference to my own. Nothing lies more at Heart on my side, than that I have given Occasion for her Majesty's Subjects formerly to complain of me, but as I have it in my Power to make ample Amends, so I am now ready to do it after what manner shall be thought convenient, provided I may be suffer'd to return Home to my own Country in Safety, with such Effects as shall be thought needful. The Necessities of the War, in all Probability, may make a Proposal of some Millions of Money, not altogether unacceptible. And tho' I am capable of maintaining my self where I am, against whatsoever Power can be brought against me, yet my Disrelish of Things that are unjust, and my Inclination to do my own Country Service, as well as close my Eyes in it, are so prevalent with me, as to make me desire your good Offices in this Affair, and tell you, that I am, with all imaginable Respect, Sir,

Your most obedient Servant, John Avery

This Letter, according to Request, was transmitted into *England*, but whether the *East India* Company thought it not adviseable to be presented to the Government, or the Ministry took no Notice of it, as an Affair too despicable, and direct coming to Terms with a Pirate and Rebel, as well as Violator of the Laws of Nations, it is not in my Power to determine; for he had no manner of Answer to it, and was left to take such Measures as he should think most conducive to his present Circumstances, which were such as not to render him contemptible. But to return to *Madagascar*, without making Enquiry into our Transactions at Home. This remarkable Deliverance of the Captain from the Machinations of his Enemies, not only gave Being to a Law, That all *French*-men whatsoever should depart that Island, but occasion'd Resolutions in *Avery* and his Council, to pursue 'em to Death, wheresoever they should find 'em. And accordingly a Fleet was equipp'd to obstruct their Commerce, and destroy their Settlements in the *North* Part of that Island; which was effected with that Vigor and Celerity, that all the Resistance could be made by the Enemy, could not

with-

...th'...'em, and they return'd from *Port St. Mary* (for that was the chief Place the *retub* East-India Company had been in Possession of ever since the Year 1654) with upwards of two Millions in Plate, Jewels, and other valuable Commodities, a fourth Part of which fell to the Captain's Share, according to the Constitution of his Government

Thus he grew in Wealth, as he grew in Years, and scarce a Week pass'd without some new adventurous Booty, so that if *Moret* could purchase his Pardon and safe Return, he had wherewithal to reside in *France*, notwithstanding their carrying their Plate, without any farther Taxes upon the Subject, and he had nothing short of the Regal Authority, but a Right to exercise it. For the Fame of his Adventures had brought all manner of People to live under his Government, and he not only coin'd Money with his own Impress upon it, but took upon him the Style, in his Edicts and Declarations, that is to be made use of by Sovereign Princes. And he not only beat the *French* out of their Dominions in that Island, but, to gratify his Ambition by not having any Thing like a Competitor, waged War with the King of the Country, that so handsomely receiv'd him at his first coming to it, and having reduced him, makes him now live under the Denomination of a Subject.

But as has been said before, all Governments are insecure, that are founded upon Violence and Rapine, and tho' he had been preserv'd from the Attempts of his pretended Friends, he had all imaginable Reason to make use of Means to defend himself from his open and avow'd Enemies, nor was he such a Stranger to the Affairs of *Europe*, how remote soever he was from the Confines of it, not to foresee that Attempts would be made to dislodge him from thence on every side, at the Conclusion of a general Peace. He therefore set himself at work to regulate, arm, and discipline his Militia, and having form'd them into several Regiments, found them to make fifteen thousand effective Men. His Preparations at Sea were nothing behind those at Land, and he saw himself Master of more than forty Vessels of War, from seven to thirty six Guns, that could be laid up on Occasion in a Bason that was defended by a Mole and a hundred Pieces of Cannon. The Forts were likewise kept in Repair, and such additional Works added to 'em, as might defeat all the Measures should be taken against him, and every Thing was put into such a Posture as not only enabled him to repel Force by Force, but deny'd the Approach of an Enemy within Reach of 'em. To go farther than this, would be to impose upon the Veracity of the Relators, as well as the Belief of the Reader, because the Person that gives these Memoirs, left the Captain when he first made Overtures for Pardon, wherefore we shall release him from any farther Enquiries, by a faithful and true Account of the Country which he is now possess'd of, and which he may take as follows.

Madagascar, or St *Lawrence*'s Island, so called because discover'd on that Day, and, according to some, from *Lawrence*, a *Portuguese*, who discover'd it in 1506. The *French*, in the Reign of *Henry* the IVth, call'd it the *Dauphine*'s Island. It is suppos'd to be the *Menuthias* of *Ptolomy*, and the *Cerne-Æthiops* of *Pliny*. It lies in the *Æthiopian* Sea, and points Westward towards *Zanguebar* and the *Caffres*, on the Coast of *Africk*. 'Tis about 50 Leagues in Length, and 80 or 100 in Breath. It is under the *Torrid Zone*, and the *Tropick* of *Capricorn*. It hath abundance of Cattle, and most of them cover'd with the Citron and Orange, or Ebony-Trees, and others, whose Wood is specify'd. The Rocks are of excellent white Marble, whence flow the best and purest Water in the World. The Country is divided into many Provinces, but those towards the *North*, are unknown to the *Europeans*. Their Villages are compos'd of moveable Houses, such as four Men can carry. Their Towns are encompass'd with Pales, and a deep Ditch six or seven Foot wide, and their Houses built of Planks. The Air is extream hot, and they have never any Snow nor Ice.

Here are several Mines of Iron and fine Steel. They have some Mines of Gold, but it is very pale. Most Sorts of precious Stones are to be found in their Rivers; and they have Store of excellent Honey, sweeter and harder than ours, resembling Sugar. They make Wine or Mead of Honey, which is the most common. Wine of Sugar, and a Sort of Cyder. They extract Oil from several Plants, Fruits, Nuts, and Grains, and have a Sort of earth, as good as the *Terra Sigillata* of *Lemnos*.

Here grows abundance of white Pepper, and precious odoriferous Wood of divers Colours. They have also Store of Canes of a vast Height and Thickness, tall and round, of which they make Pots, Bottles, Violins, and Harps, Boats that will hold two Persons, and Sedans, and take Care to give them a certain Bent, when young, to render 'em fit for their Purpose. These Canes, which they call *Bambaches*, have a Pith within, much esteem'd by the *Indians*, *Arabians* &*Persians*, & call'd the Sugar of the *Bamba's*, or *Bambothes*.

They have a very good Tobacco, and also a Sort of Hemp, whose Leaves they instead of it, which being chew'd, makes them fall asleep, and afterwards renders them extraordinary chearful, but such as are not accustom'd to it, it makes mad for three or

4 ur Days The Inhabitants are often incommoded with for its w ...h deftr ... t Corn and Fruits, but the Natives gather up ... La ft, and feed upon th m no great Plenty of common Animals, except Cru ... l s, of which ... S c at wat ... pra ... t. The Natives are of two Sorts, black and white, the eas by their Names ... t ... t ... them to be of Jewifh Extract. All of 'em go naked, h r cover their Pudenda, ... t ... of Quality have fo ... ll the Habites according to th Men or their W ... s, and ... as many as they can maintain. The Men recounce us, and puts Death as ... th Arms are Javeline Boars and Arrows. The Wemen are very difcreet, and extreme virtuous. Their Language and Writing refemble the Greek. Their Paper is of very smooth, and fi ... is made of the inner bark of a certain Tree, call'd Am ... J Ink is a fort of G m made of a Tree call'd Aravtra ... ; and their Pens made of Can ...

They believe in a God, the Creator of Heaven and Earth, who rewards the Good, and punishes the Bad he, call him Zanharre, and a r f to him but without Th er They own also that there are good and evil angels, and are mighaly afraid of the De vil, and in all their Sacrifices they throw the Devil a firft Bit, to pacify him. Their Priefts are ufually Magicians, and give 'em spells and Charms to prevent Mischiefs on. the Devil They live in Hords, like the Tartars, and to one Chief whom they call Pedvch Which Authority is many times ufurp'd by him who is most pow rful. The Hi ef Sult ... tion from this Ifland informs us, that the Princes are governed by petty Princes or Grandees, and the People are divided into feveral Ranks, tho all thefe Princes fince the Reduction of the Ifland by Capt. Perry, render an Obedience. When the Gran dees vifit one another, he who receives the Vifit, proftitutes his han fiomeft Wife to the other. And the common Peo ... entertain their Friends and Strangers in the fame Man ner. Their Grandees are much delighted with Comedies. Their Comedians, whom they chufe tiff, fhew themfelves Stoic, and acting the habit of Women, and play their Perfonal tar so decently enough.

The Air here is generally very temperate and exceeding wholefome. The oppofite Place on the Globe to Midagafcas, is the South Part of California. The Soil is extra ordinary fruitful, in many places affording all Things neceffary for the Life of Man and great Plenty. The longeft Day in the North Parts, is about 13 Hours and half, and the fhorteft in the South 9 Hours and three quarters, and the N ... ht ... to upon the ... The chiefeft Commodities of this Place, are, Rice, Hides, Wax, Gums, Chriftal, St ... Copper, Ebony and Wood of all forts towards the h rthern Part of this Ifld, is a plaisant and fertile Vall y, called correo ... which carries a River ... of Iron and Steel, and yields great Store of the Oil of Sefamus ... ne ... the ... Y ... is an excellent Medicinal Well of hot Water, which proves a ready Cure for cold Dif tempers in the Limbs. In the fame Neighbourhood, is another Stream, on whofe Tor is a remarkable Spring of ver, hot Water, tho' upwards or thirty Leagues from the S ... In the Southern Parts are moft forts of Mineral Waters, varyed Ferent both in Colo Tafte, and Quality and fome Places afford large P ... in Bitumes. In this Ifland is alfo, a River, whole Current is so exceeding hot, that there's no treading upon it, and yet the Water of that River is extreem cold.

Divers fingular Customs prevail in feveral Parts of this Ifland, particularly the te ter fift, t, ans Woman be deliver'd of a live Child, and afterwards die in Child bed, the living Child is bury'd with the dead Mother, being better (fay they) that the Chr fhould die, than live, having no Mother to look after it. The other is, their expofing their Children to wild Beafts, if brought forth upon an unlucky Day, (as they term it) or during fome unfortunate Afpects of the Planets, as their Priefts pretend to tell them and fo numerous are thefe Days they term unlucky, that almoft one half of the Year is accounted fuch, which is the Reafon the Ifland is fo thinly ftock'd with Inhabitants.

The Language here us'd, is barbarous, almoft every Province has its peculiar Dialect, yet not fo different, but that they underftand one another, fo that the Natives of this Ifland may be faid to have but one Tongue in common among 'em all

From the foregoing Defcription, may be concluded what a mighty Advantage it would be to the Crown of Great Britain, if Means could be found out by our Superiors, either to fuppress thefe Pyrates by Force, and fo get Poffeffion of this wealthy Ifland, or by Compliance with fuch Advances as have been made by the r Chief towards his Pardon which muft terminate in an entire furrendry of a Country that not only abounds with many ufeful Commodities, but, by its Extent and Strength, will add to the Renown of the Britifh Arms, which, from fuch an Accomodation, muft fhine with as great a Luftre in Africa as they have lately done in Europe. F I N I S

London Printed, and Sold by the Bookfellers 1709 Price 6 d.

Lightning Source UK Ltd.
Milton Keynes UK
UKHW020633090522
402619UK00003B/51

9 781379 743712